Growing in Grace

35 Prayer Services for Children

Growing in Grace

35 Prayer Services for Children

ALISON BERGER

TWENTY
THIRD 23rd
PUBLICATIONS

Dedication

In honor of
Blessed James Alberione, ssp, S.T.D., Founder
and Blessed Tecla Merlo, fsp, Co-Foundress
of the Daughters of St. Paul,
whose love for Scripture and the Eucharist
has profoundly influenced my spiritual journey.

The Scripture passages contained herein are from the *New Revised Standard Version of the Bible*, ©1989, by the Division of Christian Education of the National Council of Churches of Christ in the U.S.A. Used by permission. All rights reserved.

Twenty-Third Publications
A Division of Bayard
185 Willow Street
P.O. Box 180
Mystic, CT 06355
(860) 536-2611 or (800) 321-0411
www.twentythirdpublications.com

ISBN:1-58595-517-5
Library of Congress Catalog Card Number: 2005926053
Printed in the U.S.A.

Contents

Introduction

During the lifetime of St. Francis a young boy was received into the Order. The boy set his heart on learning how to pray from St. Francis. So one night he tied the cord of his habit to that of the saint, so when Francis rose to pray, he would wake up too.

However, when St. Francis awoke, he saw the cords tied together and softly undid them. Then he went into the woods to pray. After a while the boy woke up. He saw that St. Francis had already left, so he went to look for him. As he drew near to where Francis was praying, he saw a wonderful light surrounding the saint. In the light St. Francis was speaking to Jesus, Mary, and two saints.

This story, taken from *The Little Flowers of St. Francis*, continues on to tell that the young boy grew in grace and became an outstanding member of the Franciscans. After St. Francis died, the young man told the other brothers about the vision he had seen as a boy.

While the stories in *The Little Flowers* were written more for inspiration and devotion than historical accuracy, this particular story contains an important message for catechists. Consciously or not, children need and want guidance in prayer. Catechists share the privilege and responsibility of acting as guides, along with their learners' families and faith community.

Part of Your Toolbox

As I prepared these prayer services, I remembered my own experiences as a catechist. I pictured real children and used various approaches that they have enjoyed and found helpful.

Consider the prayer services offered here as part of your catechist toolbox. They are adaptable, short, and easy-to-use. All of them are based on Scripture. Most of them incorporate elements drawn from the liturgy, such as

• intercessory prayers and psalm prayers;

- liturgical rituals, e.g., presentation of the cross, renewal of baptismal promises, and blessings;
- liturgical symbols, e.g., water, candles, bread.

Some of the themes relate to the seasons and feasts of the Church year, for example, All Saints Day, Advent, Christmas, Lent, and Easter. Others invite you to pray with your children about topics relevant to the life and beliefs of a follower of Jesus:

- respect for one another
- the gift of life
- outreach to those in need
- care for the gifts of creation
- the names of God
- Jesus our Savior
- Mary the Mother of God and more.

The seasonal themes include Catholic customs and traditions with roots in different cultures, such as the Advent wreath, the Jesse tree, Las posadas, the Stations of the Cross, the rosary, and a May crowning.

Each prayer service includes an introductory note for the catechist that suggests what you will need for the service. Every service involves all the children on different levels (mind, body, heart, and so on), through opportunities to read; responses; gestures; songs; moments of silence; and activities that are part of the prayer. In addition, each service concludes with some type of response, something the children can bring away with them as an application and reminder of the prayer's theme. To further help them apply the prayer theme to their lives, an optional activity is included for each service: either a class project, a family activity, or an activity for the child to complete.

Use Your Creativity

As with any part of your religion lesson, feel free to employ your own creativity in adapting and using these prayer services with your own learners. For example, you may want to take the Scripture readings from a simple children's Bible, especially if your children are younger. On occasion you can begin the prayer service with a simple procession around your meeting space, with one of the children carrying the Bible and others carrying the other objects to be placed on the prayer table. You might want to practice the week before, and impress on the children the reverence they should show toward the Word of God. You can add gestures to some of the response prayers. You will find examples in some of the services (e.g., "The Kingdom of God"). A felt board and figures or puppets of some sort add another dimension to the Scripture readings. Use the form of guided meditation to help your learners place themselves at the scene of the Scripture passage (e.g., see "I Believe in the Holy Spirit") or to apply the reading (e.g., "Forgive One Another").

For many of the prayer services you will find a suggestion to include a relevant visual on your prayer table, e.g., a picture of Jesus, a collage of children from different countries, a baptismal candle. If these are not already included as part of the service, you can do so by discussing them with your children at some appropriate point. What is that picture or object? Why do you think we have it there today? and so on. This is something you can also have them think about as they are waiting for the lesson to begin.

The most effective use of any prayer service is to make it an integral part of your lesson, whether at the beginning to introduce the lesson; during the lesson to vary the pace or to make it a prayer lesson; or at the end to bring the subject to prayer and/or as a way to review the lesson in a prayerful atmosphere. It should not be included just for the sake of saying a prayer, any prayer.

Conclusion

Being a guide in prayer for the children you teach may seem a daunting task. This volume intends to help by providing prayer services that can be used as they are, can be adapted, or can serve as springboards for your own ideas.

May God bless us all in our efforts to grow in and guide others to a closer relationship with God.

Life Is God's Gift

Note for the Catechist

In this prayer service we pray for all those whose innocent lives are threatened, and we intend to help children learn how precious the gift of life is. Prepare a collage with magazine or newspaper pictures of people of all ages. Make paper roses, one for each child, with "Life is God's gift" printed on each. Gather around your prayer table, on which you've placed a Bible, the roses, and the collage.

Opening Prayer

Catechist	Dear God, life is a gift from you. You love and care for each of us from the very first moment of our lives. You've given every one of us—from the unborn baby to the elderly—the right to life and love. Thank you for this gift.
To the children	Because we are alive, we are able to do many things. What are some of the things we can do? (*Pause for responses.*) When we were baptized, we began a new kind of life in Jesus, as God's children. And at the end of our earthly lives, God brings us into eternal life. So life is very important, isn't it?
	Now let's do a cheer for God's gift of life!
Reader One	L is for life—God's gift.
All	L is for life—God's gift.
Reader Two	I is for "I am alive."
All	I is for "I am alive."
Reader Three	F is for "Life is forever."
All	F is for "Life is forever."
Reader Four	E is for "Life is for everyone."
All	E is for "Life is for everyone."
Reader Five	L-I-F-E, Life! Thank you, God, for the gift of life!
All	L-I-F-E, Life! Thank you, God, for the gift of life!

Gospel Reading

Reader Six   When Jesus arrived, he found that Lazarus had already been in the tomb for four days. Martha said to Jesus, "Lord, if you had been here, my brother would not have died. But even now I know that God will give you whatever you ask of him." Jesus said to her, "Your brother will rise again." Martha said to him, "I know that he will rise again in the resurrection on the last day." Jesus said to her, "I am the resurrection and the life. Those who believe in me, even though they die, will live, and everyone who lives and believes in me will never die." (Jn 11:17, 21–26)

Life Is God's Gift

This prayer poem with gestures can be recited, or sung to the tune of "My Favorite Things."

Life is a gift *(hands stretched out in front, palms up)* from God. *(raise hands upward)*
We will respect it. *(fold hands and bow head)*
Life is a great gift and *(hands stretched out, palms up)*
we will protect it. *(fold hands over heart)*
God loves each one of us right from the start. *(point to heart then around circle)*
We thank you, dear God *(fold hands)* with all of our hearts. *(both hands over heart, then stretch out toward others)*
Repeat above.
When a rose blooms, *(cup hands, palms upward)*
when a child laughs, *(put a finger on each corner of mouth and smile)*
even when we're sad. *(make a sad face)*
We'll always remember *(point hand to head)* that life is God's gift. *(raise both hands upward)*
We'll thank God and we'll be glad. *(stretch hands in front, then join hands with the persons next to you)*

Response

Give each child a paper rose as a reminder that life is God's gift. Encourage them to pray at home, that all people may respect God's gift of life.

A Prayer Hotline

Ask the children if they would like to set up a class prayer hotline. You would then ask the pastor if you can put a notice in the bulletin and/or a poster in the church letting people know they can ask your children to pray for any special intentions they have. You might want to have the children make small, simple cards that can be given to the person they're praying for. Another activity: check the church bulletin for the names of parishioners who are sick or need prayers for other situations. Send a card from your class, promising your prayers.

The Golden Rule

Note for the Catechist

This service focuses on respect and care for others. For it you will need "golden rulers" (one for each child)—strips of yellow construction paper with "Do unto others as you would have them do to you" (Mt 7:12) written on them. Gather around your prayer table on which you've placed a Bible (open to Lk 10:29–37), a candle, and the paper rulers.

Opening Prayer

Catechist   Jesus our Savior, you tell us: "Treat others as you would have them treat you." Help us learn to respect one another, no matter what our differences are. Each of us is unique, each of us is a special person. Thank you for the gifts you've given each of us.

Scripture Reading

Reader One   Jesus told a story about a man traveling from Jerusalem to Jericho. Some robbers beat him up, took his money, and left him on the road to die. One person walked by, thought the man was a robber, too, and went to the other side of the road.

All   Jesus, help us treat one another as you would.

Reader Two   Another person saw the man lying there and thought he was a beggar. He passed by, too. Then along came a man from Samaria. Now the people of Samaria and the Jewish people were not friendly to one another. But this Samaritan had a compassionate heart.

All   Jesus, help us treat one another as you would.

Reader Three	The Samaritan put medicine on the wounds of the injured man and bandaged him up. Then he took him to an inn and took care of him. Jesus asked the people who were listening to his story: "Who acted as neighbor to the man beaten by robbers?" And he said: "Go and do the same for one another." The Word of the Lord (Lk 10:29–37, paraphrased)
All	Thanks be to God.

Reflection

Catechist	Let's close our eyes and think of someone whom we look down on or ignore or treat unkindly because he or she is different from us. How would Jesus treat that person? How would we want to be treated? Say a prayer for that person, and promise Jesus that you'll do something kind for them this week.

Intercessory Prayer

Catechist	Let us offer our prayers for everyone in need.
Reader Four	For all the leaders in the Church, may they guide us wisely,
All	Lord, hear our prayer.
Reader Five	For all those who are sick in mind or body, may Jesus heal them,
All	Lord, hear our prayer.
Reader Six	For those who are in need of a home, food, and clothing, may they receive help,
All	Lord, hear our prayer.
Catechist	Loving God, please hear these petitions and grant them in the name of Jesus your Son.
All	Amen.

Closing Song

Whatsoever You Do, by Willard Jabusch (OCP Publications)

Response

Give each child one of the golden rulers as a reminder of their promise.

Setting Rules

Ask the children to help you come up with four rules about behavior in your religion classes, e.g., I will listen to each person with respect and not interrupt; I will not talk without raising my hand; etc. Type up these rules, make a copy for each child, or post a large copy in your meeting space. You might ask older children to sign their copy as a kind of covenant with the rest of the group.

All God's Children

Note for the Catechist

In this prayer service we invite the children to pray for children in difficult situations in various countries. Prepare small round pieces of construction paper (small "globes": approximately two inches in diameter), one for each child, with the name of a country in special need on each. Gather around your prayer table, on which you've placed a Bible, a large globe and/or a collage of children from different countries, and the "globes" you made.

Opening Prayer

Catechist Dear God, St. Paul tells us that we are all your children. We all belong to the same family. And, just like in our own families, what we do affects our sisters and brothers around the world. Help us do what we can to keep your family healthy and happy.

Guided Meditation

Catechist Close your eyes and breathe in and out very slowly. *(Pause)* Now picture yourself with a group of children of all ages, in the time of Jesus. You see Jesus and his disciples coming down the road. Isn't it exciting? You hope to get close to Jesus, but the adults are in the way. Suddenly Jesus says to let all the children come near him. You hear one of the disciples ask Jesus, "Who is the greatest in the kingdom of heaven?" You wait to hear what Jesus will say. What is he doing? He calls one of the children over to him and says, "Unless you change and become like little children, you will never enter the kingdom of heaven. Whoever becomes humble like this child is the greatest in the kingdom of heaven." Imagine that! Then Jesus says, "Whoever welcomes a child in my name welcomes me." Isn't that wonderful? How much Jesus loves children! (Mt 18:1–5)

Children around the World

Catechist	As we pray together, let's look at the globe and picture the children we are praying for.
Reader One	Juan and his family live in Guatemala. They have little to eat. Once Juan became so sick from hunger that he had to go to a free hospital. He was very lonely there.
All	Jesus, help us be brothers and sisters to one another.
Reader Two	Bhola lives in India. He has no books to study from. His sister doesn't even go to school because his family can't afford to send her. Bhola wants to become a teacher someday.
All	Jesus, help us be brothers and sisters to one another.
Reader Three	During the war in Kosovo Krista and her family lost everything. They lived in tents in a refugee camp in Albania. Although poor themselves, the people of Albania did what they could to help the refugees.
All	Jesus, help us be brothers and sisters to one another.
Reader Four	Kara lives in Tanzania. Her mother and father have both died of AIDS. Kara is staying with a neighbor for now, but she doesn't know what will happen to her in the future.
All	Jesus, help us be brothers and sisters to one another.
Catechist	Lord, we thank you for the gift of life, and for the gift of one another. Help us offer each other respect and kindness, for we are all your children.
All	Amen.

Response

Give each of the children a paper globe and ask them to pray this week for the children and families in the country named on their globe.

Give a Chicken or Goat

Through organizations such as Catholic Relief Services (800-736-3467) and Heifer Project International (800-422-0474), you can provide livestock to a needy family or village in another country. Contact the organization to find out the cost and the procedure. Then have a fundraiser by selling gift cards made by the children with pictures of a goat and/or baby chicks and the words: "I made a donation in your name." Each donor receives a card which he or she can give as a gift to someone.

Visit the "Forgotten State"

Note for the Catechist

This service reminds children of the millions of people who live in poverty. Prepare a large sign (like a city limits sign): Poverty USA Population: 32.3 million. Include pictures of people from different parts of the country, different ethnic backgrounds, different ages. Bring some paper cups and markers (one cup for each child). Gather around the prayer table which you have prepared with the Bible, the sign Poverty USA, and the cups and markers.

Opening Prayer

Catechist Can anyone tell me the name of the second largest state in America? *(Let the children give answers.)* The second largest state is Poverty USA. 32 million people live in poverty. That's more than all the people in Connecticut, Kentucky, Maryland, Michigan, New Jersey, and Nevada combined.

Let's pray to help people find a way out of poverty.

Loving God, we pray for all the people who live in Poverty USA. Help us share the gifts you have given us with our needy sisters and brothers. Show us how to break the bonds of poverty. We ask this in Jesus' name. Amen.

People in Need

Reader One Most days seven-year-old Peggy has no breakfast and she eats only half her lunch so she'll have something for suppertime.

All Jesus says: I was hungry and you gave me something to eat.

Reader Two Mrs. Jones, an elderly neighbor, can't afford to buy her medicine because she has to pay her heating bill.

All Jesus says: I was sick and you took care of me.

Reader Three	The people at Good Samaritan Shelter provided a temporary home for 500 homeless families last year.
All	Jesus says: I was a stranger and you took me in.
Reader Four	Mr. Little has four children. With his wage he can barely make enough to feed them and pay the bills. But he can't get another job because he doesn't have the training or education.
All	Jesus says: I needed an education and you gave me the means to get it.
Catechist	Jesus our Savior, we pray for all the families, all the children, all the elderly who struggle to make ends meet. Give them the means to live with dignity and hope. Give us the love and courage to help them in whatever way we can.
All	Amen.

Scripture Reading

Reader Five	The point is this: the one who sows sparingly will also reap sparingly, and the one who sows bountifully will also reap bountifully. Each of you must give as you have made up your mind, not reluctantly or under compulsion, for God loves a cheerful giver. And God is able to provide you with every blessing in abundance, so that by always having enough of everything, you may share abundantly in every good work. (2 Cor 9:6–8)

Response

Hand out the paper cups and markers. Have the children write Poverty USA on the cups and decorate them. Encourage them to use the cups as mite boxes during the year, to save money to help needy children.

Raising Awareness

Conduct your own mini-campaign for raising awareness about the problem of poverty in our country. Make signs with information and pictures from the CCHD website and post them in your church hall and other visible areas. Contact local shelters, soup kitchens, and other emergency service providers to find out how changes in government assistance programs are impacting them.

(Poverty USA information is from Catholic Campaign for Human Development website: www.povertyusa.org)

Respecting One Another

Note for the Catechist

This prayer service focuses on the beginning of the school year, and one virtue (among others) it's good to start the year with: respect for one another. Have materials ready to make a "ring of hearts": cardboard rings (outer diameter about seven or eight inches; ring one inch thick) with several red hearts for each, big enough (about one inch across) to cover the cardboard in a ring; plus glue. Gather around your prayer table on which you have placed a Bible (open to Mt 5), a candle, and the materials.

Opening Prayer

Catechist   Dear God, we are beginning a new year of faith formation together. As we journey through this year, we will renew old friendships and make new ones. Help us always remember to treat each person as you would treat them—with respect and kindness.

All   Amen.

Scripture Reading

Reader One   Jesus said: "You have heard that it was said, 'You shall love your neighbor and hate your enemy.' But I say to you, Love your enemies and pray for those who persecute you, so that you may be children of your Father in heaven. For if you love those who love you, what reward do you have? And if you greet only your brothers and sisters, what more are you doing than others? Be perfect as your heavenly Father is perfect." (Mt 5:43–48)

All   Be perfect as your heavenly Father is perfect.

Leader	Now let's do a cheer for the gift of respect for one another!
Reader Two	R is for real—respect is real.
All	R is for real—respect is real.
Reader Three	E is for everyone—respect is for everyone.
All	E is for everyone—respect is for everyone.
Reader Four	S is for selfless—respect is selfless.
All	S is for selfless—respect is selfless.
Reader Five	P is for patient—respect is patient.
All	P is for patient—respect is patient.
Reader One	E is for everywhere—we show respect everywhere.
All	E is for everywhere—we show respect everywhere.
Reader Two	C is for Christ—Jesus teaches us respect.
All	C is for Christ—Jesus teaches us respect.
Reader Three	T is for together—we all pull together.
All	T is for together—we all pull together.
Reader Four	R-E-S-P-E-C-T: Respect one another as Jesus would!
All	R-E-S-P-E-C-T: Respect one another as Jesus would!

Closing Prayer

Catechist	Lord Jesus, we ask you to teach us respect and care for one another, for you love each of us the same. Help us, dear Jesus, be signs of your love.
All	Amen.

Response

Hand out the materials so the children can make their ring of hearts. Invite the children to take them home as a reminder to respect one another.

Showing Respect

Ask the children to do something kind for someone with whom they find it difficult to get along or whom they look on as "different."

All You Holy Angels

Note for the Catechist

In this prayer service the children honor the ministry of angels in praising God, acting as God's messengers, and watching over us. Prepare angel-shaped prayer cards with the Prayer to the Guardian Angel on them (see closing prayer). Gather around your prayer table on which you have placed a Bible (open to Lk 2), a candle, a large picture of the Annunciation or other Scripture scene with an angel, and the prayer cards.

Opening Prayer

Catechist	God our Father, thank you for your love. Thank you for your angels, who serve you in heaven and watch over us here on earth. May they keep us safe from all harm. We ask this in Jesus' name.
All	Amen.

Scripture Reading

Reader One	In the year King Uzziah died, I saw the Lord sitting on a throne, high and lofty; and the hem of his robe filled the temple. Seraphs were in attendance above him; each had six wings. And one called to another and said: "Holy, holy, holy is the Lord of hosts." (Is 6:1–3)
All	Holy, holy, holy is the Lord of hosts!
Reader Two	In the region of Bethlehem there were shepherds living in the fields, keeping watch over their flock by night. Then an angel of the Lord stood before them, and the glory of the Lord shone around them, and they were terrified. But the angel said to them. "Do not be afraid; for see—I am bringing you good news of great joy for all the people: to you is born this day in the city of David a Savior who is the Messiah, the Lord." (Lk 2:8–11)
All	Holy, holy, holy is the Lord of hosts!

Reflection

In the gospels we read that angels ministered to Jesus in Bethlehem, in the desert, and in the garden of Gethsemane. Let's close our eyes, and in our hearts thank God for sending the angels to help us.

Intercessory Prayer

Catechist	Let us offer our prayers to God.
Reader Three	May the angels guide our Church in doing God's will.
All	Hear us, O Lord.
Reader Four	May the angels watch over families all over the world.
All	Hear us, O Lord.
Reader Five	May the angels care for the sick and the poor, especially children.
All	Hear us, O Lord.

Closing Prayer

Catechist	Let's say together the prayer to our Guardian Angel:
	Angel of God, my guardian dear, to whom God's love entrusts me here, ever this day be at my side, to light and guard, to rule and guide. Amen.

Closing Song

Angels Watching Over Me, spiritual

Response

Give each child an angel card.

Be "Angels" to Others.

Make "angel cards" for elderly persons in nursing homes or for children in hospitals. Invite the children to promise a prayer for the people who receive their cards.

The Rosary
A Gospel Prayer

Note for the Catechist

The rosary helps us reflect on the mysteries in the lives of Jesus and Mary. Prepare your prayer table with a Bible (open to Lk 1), a candle, and a statue or picture of Jesus and Mary, with a rosary placed in front of it. Make copies of the mysteries of the rosary, one for each child. You will also need copies of the Bible for the readers.

Opening Prayer

Catechist   Loving God, you sent your Son Jesus to show us the way to you. As we pray the rosary, may we learn how to become more like Jesus and Mary each day.

All   Amen.

Joyful Mysteries of the Rosary

Give the children their rosaries, and explain that after the gospel passage for each mystery is read, you will pray together one Our Father and one or more Hail Marys (as time allows).

Catechist   As we pray, let's try to picture the scene of the mystery.

       In the name of the Father and of the Son and of the Holy Spirit. Amen.

Recite the Apostles Creed

Reader One   First Joyful Mystery: The angel announces to Mary that she is chosen to be God's mother.

       The angel came to Mary and said, "Greetings, favored one! The Lord is with you.... You will conceive in your womb and bear a son, and you will name him Jesus. He will be called the Son of the Most High" (Lk 1:26–28).

16

All	Our Father... Hail Mary...
Reader Two	Second Joyful Mystery: Mary visits her cousin, St. Elizabeth.
	Mary entered the house of Zechariah and greeted Elizabeth. And Elizabeth was filled with the Holy Spirit and exclaimed with a loud cry, "Blessed are you among women, and blessed is the fruit of your womb" (Lk 1:39–42).
All	Our Father... Hail Mary...
Reader Three	Third Joyful Mystery: Jesus is born in a stable in Bethlehem.
	Joseph went to be registered with Mary, to whom he was engaged and who was expecting a child. And she gave birth to her firstborn son and wrapped him in bands of cloth, and laid him in a manger, because there was no place for them in the inn (Lk 2:1–7).
All	Our Father... Hail Mary...
Reader Four	Fourth Joyful Mystery: Mary and Joseph present Jesus in the Temple.
	When the time came for their purification according to the law of Moses, they brought him up to Jerusalem to present him to the Lord (Lk 2:22–24).
All	Our Father... Hail Mary...
Reader Five	Fifth Joyful Mystery: The boy Jesus is found in the Temple.
	When the festival was ended and they started to return, the boy Jesus stayed behind in Jerusalem, but his parents did not know it. After three days they found him in the temple, sitting among the teachers, listening to them and asking them questions (Lk 2:41–46).
All	Our Father... Hail Mary...

Closing Song

Hail Mary, Gentle Woman, by Carey Landry (OCP Publications)

Response

Give a copy of the mysteries to each child, encouraging them to pray at least one decade (or mystery) of the rosary each day.

Making Rosaries

You and the children can make rosaries that will be sent to missionaries around the world. You can even form a rosary making club. For information write to Our Lady's Rosary Makers, 4611 Poplar Level Road, Louisville, KY 40213, or call 502-968-1434.

Generous Hearts

Note for the Catechist

In many parts of the country October is a celebration of harvest time, of God's generous love, and of the fruits of the earth. On your prayer table place a Bible (open to Lk 21) surrounded by real or plastic fruits and vegetables. Prepare some small pumpkins out of orange construction paper, with the words: "Bless the Lord, O my soul."

Opening Prayer

Catechist   Loving Father, giver of all good gifts, bless the fruit of our harvest. Make our hearts fruitful with your love. Help us always remember the needs of others, especially the poor and forgotten. We ask this through Christ our Lord.

All   Amen.

Scripture Reading

Reader One   Jesus looked up and saw the rich people putting their donations into the treasury. He also saw a poor widow put in a few pennies. Jesus said, "This poor widow has put in more than all of them. They have given out of their abundance, but she out of her poverty has put in all she had to live on." (Lk 21:1–4)

All   Praise to you, Lord Jesus Christ.

Catechist   Jesus tells us that the widow gave everything she could, even though it didn't seem like much. We may not be able to give thousands of dollars to help others. But what are some things we can do? *(Pause for a few moments. Then ask the children to share their ideas.)* With the psalm we will praise God for his goodness and at the same time ask for generosity of heart.

Psalm Response

Reader Two	Bless the Lord, O my soul! O Lord my God, you are very great.
All	Bless the Lord, O my soul! (Children might accompany response with hands raised high or open wide.)
Reader Three	You set the earth on its foundations, so that it shall never be shaken. You make springs gush forth in the valley. They flow between the hills.
All	Bless the Lord, O my soul!
Reader Four	O Lord, how many are your works! The earth is full of your creatures. They all look to you to give them their food in due season. When you open your hand, they are filled with good things.
All	Bless the Lord, O my soul!

Closing Prayer

Catechist	Loving God, you are able to take our small good works and multiply them, just as you multiply the seeds, the animals, and all good things. Help us be as generous as you are with our gifts and our love. We ask this in Jesus' name.
All	Amen.

Closing Song

Praise God from Whom All Blessings Flow

Response

Give each child a paper pumpkin as a reminder of God's generous love.

Service Project

With your youngsters decide on an age-appropriate service project you can do together (cleaning up the church yard, baking cookies to raise money for Thanksgiving dinners for the needy, etc.). Obtain the necessary permissions, then pitch in!

Celebrating in Heaven

Note for the Catechist

Those of us who are following Jesus here on earth look forward to the joy of the saints in heaven. Prepare your prayer table with a Bible (open to Jn 14), a large white candle, and a very large piece of cardboard covered on one side with white paper. Draw or paste a large picture of a lamb in the center. Have sheets of 5 1/2" x 8 1/2" paper, safety scissors, glue, markers, crayons, and pencils handy.

Optional: Make cupcakes (one for each child) with messages from Scripture baked inside. Insert rolled-up messages into the batter, with the end of the message visible. Then bake the cupcakes. Place them on your prayer table.

Opening Prayer

Catechist   The saints in heaven with God are 10 zillion, zillion times happier than we are in our happiest moments here on earth. Let's thank God for the happiness he gives us and them. Let's ask the saints to pray that we may love God as much as they did.

Pause for silent prayer.

Scripture Readings

Reader One   I, John, looked, and there were so many people that no one could count them. They were standing before the throne and before the Lamb. They were robed in white, with palm branches in their hands.

All   Salvation belongs to our God and to the Lamb!

Reader Two	Then one of the elders said to me, "The Lamb will be their shepherd. He will guide them to springs of the water of life. God will wipe away every tear from their eyes." (Rev 7:14–17)
All	Salvation belongs to our God and to the Lamb!
Reader Three	Jesus said, "Do not let your hearts be troubled. In my Father's house there are many dwelling-places. If it were not so, would I have told you that I go to prepare a place for you? If I go and prepare a place for you, I will come again. I will take you to myself, so that where I am, you may be also." (Jn 14:1–3)
All	Jesus will prepare a place for us.

Activity

Have the children each draw a picture of a saint. They can cut out the pictures and glue them to the large cardboard, around the Lamb who is Jesus.

Closing Prayer

Catechist	Praise to you, loving God!
All	We praise you!
Catechist	We praise you with the sun and stars!
All	We praise you!
Catechist	We praise you with all living creatures!
All	We praise you!
Catechist	We praise you with all your angels and saints!
All	We praise you!

Response

Hand out the cupcakes.

Have a Souper Sunday

Raise money for Thanksgiving or Christmas dinners for needy families by holding a parish Souper Sunday. Children can bring in canned and packaged soups and sell tickets before and on the designated Sunday. You can prepare the delicious soup in large pots to serve to all the contributors.

Real Heroes and Heroines

Note for the Catechist

We honor the saints who show us how to follow in Jesus' footsteps. On your prayer table place a Bible (open to Mt 5), a large white candle, and pictures of different saints (look on the Internet and in your parish/school library). Type or print on small cards (one for each child) this prayer of St. Teresa of Avila: "Christ has no body now but yours. Yours are the hands through which he does good." Before the prayer service point out the pictures of the saints to the children.

Opening Prayer

Catechist	Loving God, ever since Jesus rose from the dead, you have called holy men and women to follow in his footsteps. May we honor the saints. We ask them to pray for us, so we can love you as much as they did.
All	Amen.

Scripture Reading

Reader One	You are the salt of the earth. If salt has lost its taste, how can its saltiness be restored? It is no longer good for anything but is thrown out and trampled on.
All	We are the salt of the earth!
Reader Two	You are the light of the world. A city built on a hill cannot be hidden. No one lights a lamp and puts it under a bushel basket. They put it on a lamp-stand to light up the whole house. In the same way, let your light shine before others. Then they may see the good you do and give glory to your Father in heaven. (Mt 5:13–16)
All	We are the light of the world!

Litany of the Saints

Catechist	Now we will say a special prayer to the saints, asking them to help us be more like Jesus.
Reader Three	Holy Mary, Mother of God
All	Pray for us.
Reader One	St. Peter and St. Paul
All	Pray for us.
Reader Two	St. Joseph
All	Pray for us.
Reader Three	St. Francis of Assisi and St. Catherine of Siena
All	Pray for us.
Reader One	St. Agnes and St. Augustine
All	Pray for us.
Reader Two	St. Bernadette and St. Dominic Savio
All	Pray for us.
Reader Three	St. Thérèse and St. Katharine Drexel
All	Pray for us.
Reader Four	St. Juan Diego and St. Elizabeth Ann Seton
All	Pray for us.
Reader One	(Add the name of your parish or school's patron saint)
All	Pray for us.
Reader Two	All you holy saints of God
All	Pray for us.

Closing Song

We Are the Light of the World, Jean Anthony Greif (Vernacular Hymns Publishing Co)

Response

Give each child one of the cards with the prayer of St. Teresa. Encourage them to think of the words often during the month.

All Saints Day Poster

Make a poster (or mural) for All Saints Day. It could include drawings, poems, pictures of your children and their family members, and so on. Let the kids be creative.

Thanksgiving: Gifts of Creation

Note for the Catechist

Through this prayer service we thank God for all the gifts of creation. Make several signs (one for each child in your religion class) with one of these phrases on each sign: I am water, I am air, I am tree, I am earth, I am animal. Photocopy the children's words below (after the Scripture reading) and glue the appropriate words on the back of each sign. For this service gather around your prayer table, on which are placed a Bible, a large nature scene, and the signs.

Opening Prayer

Catechist   Loving God, your creation is filled with so many beautiful and wonderful gifts. Thank you for the water, earth, and air, for animals, birds, and fish, for trees, flowers, and plants. May we be good stewards of your creation.

All   Amen.

Scripture Reading

Reader One   In the beginning God created the heavens and the earth.... God said, "Let the earth put forth vegetation: plants yielding seed and fruit trees of every kind." Then God said, "Let the waters bring forth swarms of living creatures, and let birds fly above the earth."

Reader Two   Then God said, "Let the earth bring forth living creatures of every kind: cattle and creeping things and wild animals on the earth." Then God said, "Let us make humankind—men and women—in our image." God blessed them and God said to them, "Be fruitful and multiply." (Gen 1:1–28)

Catechist   God made everything on earth and in the heavens very special. Together we will thank him for some of these gifts.

(Hand out the signs. Tell the children that when you say a gift—for example, I am air—all the children with that sign will say their verse along with you.)

Catechist   I am water.

Children	I come to earth as rain. I praise God by bringing life to living things. I quench the thirst of each person, of animals, and of plants. Please keep me pure and clear for everyone.
Catechist	I am air.
Children	I am everywhere, though you cannot see me. I praise God by carrying sound and light to you. I enable you to breathe. Please keep me fresh and unpolluted.
Catechist	I am earth.
Children	I was formed by God many thousands of years ago. I praise God by bringing forth trees and plants and fruit, food for you and other living things. Please keep me and my children clean and beautiful.
Catechist	I am tree.
Children	You sit in my shade, you eat my fruit, you use my wood in your homes. I praise God in all these ways. Please keep me safe from fire and from being wasted.
Catechist	I am animal.
Children	I play on the earth and in the sea and sky. I praise God with my beauty. I provide food for you. Please keep me safe from abuse and extinction.
All	Thank you, loving God, for all these gifts!

Closing Prayer

Catechist	God our Creator, you have given us life and the ability to enjoy the beautiful things you have made. Help us respect your gifts. May we always have a thankful heart. We ask this through Jesus your Son and our Savior.
All	Amen.

Closing Song

We Will Praise You, Tom Kendzia (Lead Us to the Water, OCP Publications)

Response

Ask the children to write their own thank you prayers.

A Recycled Art Auction

Invite the children to collect recyclable items such as plastic bottles, paper bags, etc. Provide markers, glue, sequins, and other craft and art materials, and let them use their gifts and talents to create sculptures, miniature towns, and craft items to be auctioned off. The proceeds can go toward a local food pantry or the parish. Have the auction after a weekend Mass, selling the art pieces with bidding starting around 25¢. You'll have lots of fun, while involving the children in a practical service project.

A Jesse Tree Celebration

Note for the Catechist

The Jesse tree is an ancient Advent custom that connects us with our ancestors in the faith. It also helps us prepare for the celebration of the birth of Jesus, the Expected One.

You will need a large tree branch secured in a bucket of wet sand; sheets of white paper; a hole punch; safety scissors; pencils, markers, or crayons; thread or ribbon. You might wish to extend the making of the Jesse Tree through all your Advent sessions, then use the prayer service at the end.

Opening Prayer

Catechist   During Advent we think about all the people in the Bible who helped prepare the way for Jesus our Savior. Making the Jesse Tree is one way of remembering them. Let's ask these holy men and women to help us prepare our hearts for Jesus' birth.

Litany

Invite the children to respond "Pray for us" after each petition.

Reader One   Adam and Eve, our first parents...

Reader Two   Noah who built the ark...

Reader Three   Abraham and Sarah who followed God's call into a strange land...

Reader Four   Joseph who saved his people during a famine...

Reader Five   Moses and Miriam who led the Israelites out of bondage...

Reader Six   Ruth who teaches us the virtue of loyalty...

Reader Seven   David, great king of Israel...

Reader Eight   Isaiah and all God's prophets...

Reader Nine	Joseph, foster father of Jesus...
Reader Ten	Mary, mother of Jesus...
Catechist	Loving God, in every age you sent holy men and women to lead your people. As we prepare for the coming of Jesus, help us listen to your Word with the same love and faithfulness they had.
All	Amen.

Making the Tree

Hand out the paper, pencils, etc. Assign each child a symbol to draw for one of the biblical figures. Provide samples if needed. For younger children, draw the outlines of the symbols ahead of time. When all have finished coloring and cutting out their symbols, punch a hole and thread a piece of ribbon or thread at the top of each symbol and hang them on the Jesse Tree. A list of suggested symbols follows.

Adam and Eve: apple, tree

Noah: ark, rainbow

Abraham and Sarah: tent

Jacob: ladder with angels

Joseph: coat of many colors

Moses and Miriam: baby basket in water

Ruth: sheaf of wheat

David: harp, crown

Isaiah: scroll

Esther: crown

St. Joseph: carpenter's tools

Mary: lily or large M with a crown

Family Scripture Reading

During Advent invite the families of your children to read together passages from Scripture that tell the stories of the biblical figures whose symbols are part of the Jesse tree. They may prefer to read the stories from a complete Children's Bible, especially if they have young children.

An Advent Wreath Ceremony

Note for the Catechist

The Advent wreath has a special significance. The green circle represents God's eternity. The candles are a symbol of the spirit of Advent, one of hope and waiting. If you don't have a wreath, you and/or your youngsters can make one. Make a circle out of wire, then use string or twine to attach evergreen branches to the wire. You will also need four candles (three purple or dark blue and one pink; or three white and one pink) with holders. On each Sunday of Advent, gather around the Advent wreath to light the candle(s) and pray together.

Opening Prayer

Catechist   Loving God, we prepare to celebrate again the coming of your Son Jesus on earth and into our hearts. Bless this Advent wreath. May it be a symbol of our hope in your everlasting love and faithfulness. We ask this in Jesus' name.

All   Amen.

Scripture Reading

Reader One   In the sixth month the angel Gabriel was sent by God to a town in Galilee called Nazareth. He went to visit a young girl whose name was Mary. The angel said to her, "Hail, full of grace! The Lord is with you!"

Reader Two   "Do not be afraid, Mary, for God loves you very much. You will conceive and bear a son and you will name him Jesus. He will be called Son of the Most High."

Reader Three   Then Mary said, "I am the servant of the Lord. Let it be done to me according to your word." (Lk 1:26–35)

First Sunday of Advent

Light the first purple candle and say this prayer:

Reader One   Jesus, please take care of us. May we love you more and more.

All   Bless us and all your people. Amen.

Second Sunday of Advent

Light the first and second purple candles and say this prayer:

Reader Two   You bring joy to us, Jesus. Let us bring joy to others.

All   Bless us and all your people. Amen.

Third Sunday of Advent

Light the two purple candles and the pink candle and say this prayer:

Reader Three   We praise and bless you, Jesus, for your goodness to us. Help us treat others as you would.

All   Bless us and all your people. Amen.

Fourth Sunday of Advent

Light all four candles and say this prayer:

Reader Four   Mary, help us learn from you to be thankful for all God's gifts, especially for the gift of his Son Jesus.

All   Bless us and all your people. Amen.

Closing Song

O Come, O Come, Emmanuel, or another Advent song

Response

Give each child a copy of the prayers they can say each week with their family.

Straws for Jesus

Prepare a simple "manger" (you can decorate a shoe box) and put straw next to it. Put it on your prayer table. Tell the children they can place a few pieces of straw in Jesus' manger for every good act they've done during the week. They might even want to make their own mangers to use at home.

Las Posadas
An Advent Celebration

Note for the Catechist

Posada is a Spanish word that means shelter. Las Posadas (lahs po SA das) celebrates Mary and Joseph's journey and search for shelter in Bethlehem. On each of the nine nights before Christmas, beginning December 16th, processions of family and friends go from house to house (or from room to room in a large house), by prearranged invitation. Children carrying figures of Mary and Joseph lead the procession. At each door they pause to sing *Pedida de las Posadas*, saying they are tired and cold and asking for lodging.

You might arrange a simple version of the Posadas for your group. Explain the meaning of the custom. Invite the children to pray for homeless people. Then separate the children into two groups. One group of children can carry the figures of Joseph and Mary from a nativity set. They can process from room to room in your parish school building or hall. At each door they might sing or say part of the *Pedida de las Posadas* (in English or Spanish: see the words on the next page) or sing Christmas carols.

The other group will play the innkeepers. Each time the first group comes to a door and sings for shelter, the innkeeper opens the door a crack. He or she refuses to let the strangers in. When the children reach the last door, the innkeeper lets them in. The children set the figures of Joseph and Mary in a place of honor, decorated beforehand. You might conclude the celebration with a few more carols, or a game, or even the breaking of a piñata.

Pedida de las Posadas

Afuera	En el nombre del cielo les pido posada, pues no puede andar mi esposa amada.
Adentro	Aquí no es mesón: sigan adelante, yo no debo abrir no sea algún tunante.
Afuera	Venimos cansados desde Nazareth; yo soy carpintero de nombre José.
Adentro	No me importa el nombre: déjenme dormir, porque ya les dije, que no he de abrir.
Afuera	Mi esposa es María, es reina del cielo, y madre va a ser del Divino Verbo.
Adentro	¿Eres tú José? ¿Tú esposa es María? Entren peregrinos: no los conocía.
Afuera	Dios pague, señores, su gran caridad y les colme el cielo de felicidad.
Adentro	Dichosa la casa que alberga este día, a la virgen pura, la hermosa María.

Looking for Shelter

Group One	In heaven's name I beg you for a room. My beloved wife cannot walk any further.
Group Two	This is not an inn; be on your way. I can't let you in, you might be a scoundrel.
Group One	We come from Nazareth, and we're very tired. I am a carpenter. My name is Joseph.
Group Two	Your name doesn't matter. Let me sleep. I've already told you that I won't let you in.
Group One	My wife is Mary. She is the queen of heaven. She will be mother of the Son of God.
Group Two	Is that you, Joseph? Is that your wife Mary? Come in, pilgrims, I didn't recognize you.
Group One	May God repay you for your great kindness. May heaven bless you with much happiness.
Group Two	Our house is blessed for today it gives shelter to the holy Virgin and to her Son.

We Bring Our Gifts

Note for the Catechist

The three wise men or kings teach us about offering gifts to the Child Jesus as part of our Advent/Christmas celebration. Before your session cut small treasure chests out of gold or yellow construction paper, one for each child. On the back write: What will I give him? I'll give him my heart.

Prepare your prayer table with the Bible (open to Mt 2), an incense burner, a small container of perfumed oil, and a box covered in gold paper (to represent frankincense, myrrh, and gold). Place the treasure chests on the table as well.

Opening Song

We Three Kings of Orient Are, traditional

Opening Prayer

Catechist	With the wise men we seek the Child Jesus in our hearts and in our lives. Let us be ready for his coming by offering him some special gift of love. Dear God, bless our Advent preparations. May they bring us closer to you.
All	Amen.

Scripture Reading

Reader One	In the time of King Herod, after Jesus was born in Bethlehem of Judea, wise men from the East came to Jerusalem. They asked, "Where is the child who has been born king of the Jews?"
All	What will I give him? I'll give him my heart.
Reader Two	Then Herod secretly called for the wise men. He learned from them the exact time when the star had appeared.
All	What will I give him? I'll give him my heart.

Reader Three	When they had heard the king, the wise men set out. Ahead of them went the star that they had seen at its rising. It stopped over the place where the child was.
All	What will I give him? I'll give him my heart.
Reader Four	On entering the house the wise men saw the child with Mary his mother. They knelt down and paid him homage.
All	What will I give him? I'll give him my heart.
Reader Five	Then opening their treasure chests, they offered him gifts of gold, frankincense, and myrrh. (Mt 2:1–12)

(The catechist or the reader should lift the three objects representing the gifts of the wise men, one by one.)

All	What will I give him? I'll give him my heart.
Catechist	Let us all stop a moment to think about what we can give Jesus at Christmas time. *(Pause for a few moments of silence.)*

Closing Prayer

Catechist	Loving God, we praise and thank you for sending your Son Jesus to show us your love. Help us return that love with deeds of kindness.
All	Amen.

Closing Song

O Come All Ye Faithful, or another carol.

Response

Give each child one of the treasure chests you prepared, as a reminder to return Jesus' love.

Buy Some Bees

Start a service project to buy something for a poverty-stricken village as part of a livestock or farm project, through Samaritan's Purse. Raise money to purchase a goat or donkeys, a hive of honey bees, water filters, education for one child, or hot meals. Keep a laminated picture of what you are raising money for in your meeting space. For more information, check out www.samaritanspurse.org, or call (828) 262-1980.

Let Peace Begin with Me

Note for the Catechist

Peace in the world begins with each one of us, and here the children pray for that peace. You'll need five pieces of white construction paper (at least 5.5" x 8.5"). On each piece write one letter of the word "anger" on one side and one letter of the word "peace" on the other (P should be on the back of A, E on the back of N, A on the back of G, and so forth). Also prepare prayer cards with copies of St. Francis' Peace Prayer.

On your prayer table place a Bible (opened to Lk 6), a candle, and the letters you've prepared, propped up with the word "anger" spelled out.

Opening Prayer

Catechist	Loving God, you called St. Francis of Assisi to be a great peacemaker. With his life even more than with his words he showed people how to imitate Jesus' love and forgiveness. Help us follow his example so we may be peace-makers, too. We ask this in Jesus' name.
All	Amen.

Gospel Reading

Reader	Jesus said, "No good tree bears bad fruit, nor again does a bad tree bear good fruit; for each tree is known by its own fruit. Figs are not gathered from thorns, nor are grapes picked from a bramble bush. The good person out of the good treasure of the heart produces good, and the evil person out of evil treasure produces evil; for it is out of the abundance of the heart that the mouth speaks." (Lk 6:43–45)

Reflection

Catechist	Let us each ask ourselves: Is there peace in my heart? Do I try to keep peace with others? What does peace mean to me? (*Discuss these with the children. If*

34

you have younger children, you might ask them to draw a picture showing what peace means to them.) Now let's pray that peace will begin with each one of us.

Prayer Petitions

As each reader offers a petition, he/she will turn over one letter of the word "anger," so that at the end the word "peace" will show.

Reader One	When I am angry, help me forgive.
All	Let peace begin with me.
Reader Two	When I hurt others, help me say I'm sorry.
All	Let peace begin with me.
Reader Three	When I see someone sad, help me cheer them up.
All	Let peace begin with me.
Reader Four	When my friends are arguing, help me bring peace.
All	Let peace begin with me.
Reader Five	When there is hurt in my family, help me bring love.
All	Let peace begin with me.

Closing Prayer

Catechist	St. Francis, you loved Jesus so much that you tried your best to be like him. Pray for us, that we may love Jesus and love one another—not only in what we say but in the way we act. Help us keep peace in our hearts and give that peace to one another.
All	Amen.

Closing Song

Prayer of St. Francis, Sebastian Temple (OCP Publications)

Response

Give each child a copy of St. Francis' Prayer and invite them to pray it each day.

Peace Balloons

Invite the children to make these small peace balloons that can help relieve stress in a tense situation. Show them how to stretch their balloons by blowing them up, then letting the air out. Fill each balloon with one-third cup of flour or play sand. Tie the end of the balloon in a knot and cut off the extra. The children can decorate their balloons with funny faces or designs. When they are upset or angry, squeezing the balloon will help reduce their stress and give them time to think about how they will respond to the situation.

Hopes and Dreams

Note for the Catechist

The beginning of the new year is an appropriate time for the children to look at their hopes and dreams and what they can do to achieve them. Prepare your prayer corner with a Bible (open to 1 Cor 12), a candle, and a collage of persons of all ages doing different things (e.g., a doctor, a singer, a child flying a kite, a family, and so on). You will also need sheets of 8.5" x 11" heavy white paper, construction paper of different colors, pencils, markers, crayons, safety scissors, and glue. Before the prayer service point out the collage to the children.

Opening Prayer

Catechist   Loving God, today we are going to look at the hopes and dreams we have in our hearts. Please bless these hopes, and bless us as we pray to you in Jesus' name.

All   Amen.

Scripture Reading

Reader One   Each of us has a different dream about what we would like to do or be. St. Paul talks about some of these.

Reader Two   You are the body of Christ and each of you are members of it. God has given the church apostles, prophets, and teachers. God has given us deeds of power, gifts of healing, ways of helping others, and different kinds of leaders. But the greatest gift is love. (1 Cor 12:27–31; 13:13)

All   The greatest gift is love.

Expressing Dreams

Now pass out the materials you brought and ask the children to draw, make a design, or write about at least one of their dreams (something they hope to be or do). When most of the children have finished, invite them, one at a time, to share their dreams. When all the children have had a chance to share, talk about what we can do to reach our dreams. You can give an example of your own to help get them started. Coach them a little if necessary, but let them give their suggestions freely. Then pray this prayer:

Psalm Prayer

Catechist   Dear God, we offer you the drawings and writings that express our dreams. Give us the wisdom to follow our dreams.

Reader Three   Wisdom is radiant and unfading, and she is easily found by those who love her.

All   Love for God is the beginning of wisdom.

Reader Four   If we rise early to seek wisdom, we will have no difficulty, for she will be found sitting at the gate.

All   Love for God is the beginning of wisdom.

Reader One   Obeying wisdom's laws brings us near to God.

All   Love for God is the beginning of wisdom.

Closing Prayer

Catechist   Dear God, you gently bless the dreams of those who trust in you. You help them come true, if they are what is best for us. May we not be afraid to follow our dreams, as Jesus did. We ask this in Jesus' name.

All   Amen.

Response

Invite the children to take home what they drew or wrote about their dream, and keep it somewhere as a reminder.

Special Visitor

Invite your pastor, a parent, a religious brother or sister, or a lay minister to come and talk to the children about their vocations and dreams.

For Christian Unity

Note for the Catechist

This prayer service helps children learn to pray for unity among Christians. Prepare a large cardboard circle with a red heart in the center. Provide sheets of white construction paper, pencils, safety scissors, and glue. On your prayer table place a Bible (open to Jn 17), a candle, and the cardboard circle.

Opening Prayer

Catechist	Loving God, during this month we celebrate the week of prayer for Christian Unity. Help all of us who believe in Jesus to respect and love one another. May we all be one in faith, hope, and love for you. We ask this in Jesus' name.
All	Amen.

Scripture Reading

Reader One	I, Paul, beg you to lead a life worthy of the calling to which you have been called. Be humble, gentle, and patient. Bear with one another in love. Make every effort to keep the unity of the Spirit in the bond of peace. (Eph 4:1–3)
All	Jesus, help us be brothers and sisters to one another.
Reader Two	There is one body and one Spirit, just as you were called to the one hope of your calling. We believe in one Lord, one faith, one baptism, one God and Father of all. (Eph 4:4–5)
All	Jesus, help us be brothers and sisters to one another.
Reader Three	Jesus prayed: "Holy Father, protect them in your name that you have given me. May they be one, as we are one." (Jn 17:11)
All	Jesus, help us be brothers and sisters to one another.

Reader Four	"I ask this not only for these followers, but also for those who will believe in me through their word. As you, Father, are in me and I am in you, may they also be in us." (Jn 17:20–21)
All	Jesus, help us be brothers and sisters to one another.

Closing Prayer

Catechist	Jesus, you prayed for unity among your followers. May we live according to your gospel of peace and love. Help us live united with our brothers and sisters, in our families, neighborhood, and the world.
All	Amen.

Closing Song

They Will Know We Are Christians by Our Love, Peter Scholtes (F.E.L. Publications, Ltd.)

Response

Hand out pieces of construction paper, pencils, and safety scissors. Ask the children to trace one of their hands on the paper, then cut out the shape. Invite them to write their names on their paper hands. Glue all the hands around the heart on the cardboard circle. While you are gluing the hands, sing *They Will Know We Are Christians*.

For Christian Unity

Contact your pastor or your parish liaison for ecumenical events and ask how the children in your group can contribute to the Week of Prayer for Christian Unity, as well as other ecumenical events or projects.

Presentation of the Cross

Note for the Catechist

This presentation of the cross is based on a rite that is part of the RCIA process for catechumens. It emphasizes the symbolism of the cross for us as followers of Jesus. Prepare your prayer table with the Bible (open to Lk 23:33), a candle, a standing crucifix or cross, and small crosses or crucifixes (these can be made out of heavy paper or twigs or purchased at a religious goods store). Play reflective background music.

Opening Prayer

Catechist   Jesus, by your cross and resurrection you have set us free. You are our loving Savior. Help us remember this every time we sign ourselves with the cross.

Together let us make the sign of the cross: In the name of the Father and of the Son and of the Holy Spirit.

All   Amen.

Scripture Readings

Reader One   St. Paul wrote: "The message about the cross is foolishness to those who do not believe. To us who are being saved it is the power of God." (1 Cor 1:18)

All   We adore you, O Christ, and we bless you. By your holy cross you have redeemed the world.

Reader Two	When they came to the place that is called The Skull, they crucified Jesus there with the criminals. One was on his right and one on his left. Then Jesus said, "Father, forgive them. They do not know what they are doing." (Lk 23:33–34)
All	We adore you, O Christ, and we bless you. By your holy cross you have redeemed the world.
Reader Three	Jesus said to the repentant thief, "Today you will be with me in Paradise." (Lk 23:43)
All	We adore you, O Christ, and we bless you. By your holy cross you have redeemed the world.

Signing with the Cross

Catechist	Children, Jesus calls you to be his friends. Always be faithful to him. Let the sign of the cross remind you of Jesus and how much he loves you.

Trace the sign of the cross over each child's forehead:

Catechist	May Jesus bless your mind, thoughts, and imaginations, to know him better.
Then hands:	May Jesus bless your actions and do good through you.
Then heart:	May Jesus bless your heart so you will love him more and more.

Were You There, African-American Spiritual

Response

Give each child a cross to keep with them.

Stations of the Cross Booklets

Have your children prepare their own Stations of the Cross booklets. They can cut out pictures from magazines, old calendars, and so on, that interpret each station for them. Then they can write their own reflections and prayers to go with each picture. Younger children can draw or color their own stations.

The children could also do this project in groups. Or the older children could share their reflections and prayers with the younger ones, and vice versa.

Forgive One Another

Note for the Catechist

This prayer service focuses on our need to forgive one another as God forgives us. Prepare your prayer table with a Bible (open to Mt 18), a candle, and cards cut in the shape of teddy bears (for children a symbol of love and caring), with the words: "Forgive one another as I have forgiven you" printed on them.

Opening Prayer

Catechist   Merciful Father, you love us no matter how many times we offend you. Help us show that same kind of forgiveness to one another, truly and from the heart. We ask this in Jesus' name.

All   Amen.

Scripture Reading

Reader One   Then Peter came and said to Jesus, "Lord, if another member of the church sins against me, how often should I forgive? As many as seven times?" Jesus said to him, "Not seven times but seventy times seven times" (Mt 18:21–22).

All   Jesus, help us forgive one another.

Reader Two   "I beg you to lead a life worthy of the calling to which you have been called, with all humility and gentleness, with patience, bearing with one another in love." (Eph 4:1–3)

Catechist	Let's close our eyes now. Picture yourself in a place where you feel happy. *(Pause.)* Picture Jesus welcoming you there. *(Pause.)* Talk to him about those persons you may have offended, and ask his forgiveness. *(Pause.)* Now talk to him about people who have hurt you or whom you find it hard to get along with. Ask Jesus to help you show them love and forgiveness. *(Pause.)*
Catechist	Loving God, we want to bring peace and forgiveness everywhere in Jesus' name. Bless us as we pray:
All	Jesus, help us forgive one another.
Catechist	For the times we use unkind words,
All	Jesus, help us forgive one another.
Catechist	For the times we don't offer to help someone,
All	Jesus, help us forgive one another.
Catechist	For the times when we ignore someone or treat them as different,
All	Jesus, help us forgive one another.
Catechist	For the times when we find it hard to forgive,
All	Jesus, help us forgive one another.
Catechist	Let us pray together the prayer Jesus taught us.
All	Our Father...
Catechist	Now let us offer each other a sign of peace.

Closing Song

Let There Be Peace on Earth, Sy Miller and Jill Jackson (Jan-Lee Music)

Response

Give each of the children one of the bear cards. Suggest that, if they have someone they need to be reconciled with, they write a note on the card, sign it, and give it to the other person.

The Prodigal Son

Invite the children to write and act out a simple, modern version of the parable of the prodigal son. Or use sock puppets to act out the gospel story.

Vine and Branches

Note for the Catechist

In this prayer service the children reflect on their relationship with Jesus. Prepare a large piece of white felt to make a banner, plus a green vine with many branches which you glue to the banner. Write "I am the vine, you are the branches" on the banner. Cut green leaves out of construction paper. Explain to the children that for each act of kindness, forgiveness, and so on, they can write "yes" to God on the back of a leaf and glue it to the banner.

Use this prayer service each week during Lent, and have your children add their leaves to the vine. The banner can hang in front of the prayer table or in another appropriate place.

Opening Prayer

Catechist	Jesus, you said, "I am the vine, you are the branches." During this lenten season we want to grow closer to you by being kind, forgiving, and prayerful. Please bless us, Jesus.
All	Amen.

Scripture Reading

Reader One	Jesus said, "I am the vine and you are the branches. Live in me as I live in you. The branch cannot bear fruit by itself, unless it is attached to the vine. Neither can you unless you live in me."
All	You are the vine, we are the branches.
Reader Two	"I am the vine and you are the branches. If you live in me and my words live in you, ask for what you wish and it will be done for you."
All	You are the vine, we are the branches.

Reader Three	"As the Father has loved me, so I have loved you. Live in my love. If you keep my commandments you will live in my love. I have said these things so my joy may be in you and your joy may be complete." (Jn 15:4–11)
All	You are the vine, we are the branches.

Invite the children to attach their leaves to the vine. You can play soft instrumental music as they are doing this. After the children have finished, ask them to stand.

Intercessory Prayer

Divide the children into two groups (example: left side and right side of the room). Ask Group One to pray the first part of the prayer, and Group Two to pray the second part.

Group One	Jesus, the true vine, bless the Church.
Group Two	May it always be true to you.
Group One	Jesus, bless those who proclaim your Word.
Group Two	Give them courage and perseverance.
Group One	Jesus, bless our families and friends.
Group Two	Draw them closer to your heart.
Catechist	Jesus, hear these petitions we bring to you. Please grant them for our growth in holiness.

Closing Song

O Sacred Head, Surrounded, or another lenten song

Response

Remind the children that in each session they can add a leaf to the vine for each good deed they do during the week.

Prayer Partners

In one of your sessions encourage your children to write a note to someone in the parish who is homebound. (Your social ministry committee or pastor will have the names and addresses of these parishioners.) In the note the children can describe one thing they learned recently and ask the person to exchange prayers with them.

We're on Jesus' Team

Note for the Catechist

Children want to belong, and whose team better than Jesus'? Prepare a collage of different kinds of teams (especially with kids): baseball, scientists, drama, games, helping other people, and so on. Cut the collage into several pieces, and put a piece of double-sided tape on the back of each. Prop a large piece of cardboard in a visible place. Gather around the prayer table on which you've placed the Bible and the pieces of the collage.

Opening Dialogue

Catechist	Do you belong to any teams? What kind? What would happen to your team if each member looked out only for himself or herself? Let's ask Jesus to help us be good members of his team, working together to build up the kingdom of God.

Scripture Reading

Reader One	In Matthew's gospel Jesus says: "Do not worry about what you are going to eat or drink. Your heavenly Father knows that you need all these things. But first seek the kingdom of God. Then everything else will be given to you."
All	Jesus, may we follow you.
Reader Two	Help us be good members of your team, Jesus. Show us how we can help build up your kingdom.
All	Jesus, may we follow you.
Catechist	What makes a person a good team member? *(Pause for answers.)* Now, close your eyes. Imagine that Jesus is coming toward you and inviting you to be on his team. What kind of qualities would he look for in a team member? Talk to him about it. *(Pause for answers.)*

Intercessory Prayer

Catechist	Loving God, we ask for the gifts we need to work together so "thy kingdom may come." In this spirit we pray:
All	Your kingdom come.
Reader Three	Jesus, you promised to be with those who pray in your name,
All	Be with us as we work for your kingdom.
Reader Four	Jesus our Teacher, help us please God in our thoughts, words, and actions,
All	So we may be open to the voice of the Holy Spirit.
Reader Five	Jesus our King, lead us and we will follow
All	So we all can belong to your team.
Together	Our Father...

Activity

Hand out the collage pieces to the children. They need to fit them together on the cardboard. Tell them not to attach the pieces until everyone has found the right spot for their piece. Children without puzzle pieces can help the others with suggestions and encouragement. Set a time limit to make the activity more challenging.

Closing Prayer

Catechist	You speak to us often, Jesus, our Savior, if only we would listen. Thank you for calling us to follow in your footsteps. Teach us how to be loyal, honest, respectful (add any other qualities the children named). Stay with us always.
All	May we always listen to your voice, risen Savior. Amen.

Response

Encourage the children to think about and write down what it takes to make a good team member. How can they acquire or grow in these qualities?

An Easter Prayer Tree

Make a class Easter egg prayer tree. Place a large branch in a plant container filled with sand. Hand out strips of paper and markers, and ask the children to write short messages on them, promising prayers. For example, they could write: I will say a Hail Mary for you. Have the children sign their first name, if appropriate. Place each message in a colored plastic egg. Fasten the eggs to the "tree" with string. Then present the Easter egg tree to children in a hospital, to a hospice for AIDS patients, or to a senior center.

Blessing with Water

Note for the Catechist

Blessing with water reminds us of our baptism. Prepare your prayer table with a Bible (open to Jn 4), a baptismal candle, a bowl of water, and an evergreen branch. You will also need a copy of the Bible for the Scripture reading. Have a real or paper taper for each child as a reminder of their baptism.

Opening Prayer

Catechist	We use water for many different things, don't we? *(Ask the children to name some.)* Each of us was baptized with water as a sign of our new life in Christ.
	Let us pray now. God, our loving Creator, through baptism you have given us new life. As we renew the promises made at baptism, help us remember our call to follow Jesus every day.
All	Amen.

Renewal of Baptismal Promises

Catechist	Do you reject sin so you can live as God's children?
Response	I do.
Catechist	Do you believe in God who has created us?
Response	I do.
Catechist	Do you believe in Jesus Christ who has redeemed us?
Response	I do.
Catechist	Do you believe in the Holy Spirit who makes us holy?
Response	I do.

Catechist	Do you promise to be faithful as a follower of Jesus?
Response	I do.
Catechist	Do you promise to help others in need?
Response	I do.

Scripture Reading

Reader One	A Samaritan woman came to draw water. Jesus said to her, "Give me a drink." The Samaritan woman said to him, "How is it that you, a Jew, ask a drink of me, a woman of Samaria?"
Reader Two	Jesus answered her, "If you knew the gift of God, and who is saying to you, 'Give me a drink,' you would have asked him. He would have given you living water." The woman said to him, "Sir, you have no bucket, and the well is deep. Where do you get that living water?"
Reader Three	Jesus said to her, "Everyone who drinks of this water will be thirsty again, but those who drink of the water that I will give them will never be thirsty. The water that I will give will become a spring of water gushing up to eternal life." (Jn 4:7–14)

Prayer over the Water

Catechist	Praise to you, all powerful God, for you have created water to cleanse and give life. Through this blessing with water, fill our hearts with the Spirit of your love.
All	Amen.

Dip the evergreen branch in the water and sprinkle the children with it.

Closing Song

You Have been Baptized in Christ, Carey Landry (OCP Publications)
Lead Us to the Water: Dismissal, Tom Kendzia (Lead Us to the Water, OCP Publications)

Response

Give each child one of the tapers to take home. Invite them to keep the real or paper candles in a special place as a reminder of their baptism.

Make Butterflies

Make small butterflies from wallpaper samples, clothespins, and pipe cleaners. Then bring them to children or adults who are hospitalized or confined to their homes. You might have the children include a brief note about the symbolism of the butterfly, or simply tell them how butterflies represent the cycle of life, death, and resurrection.

Jesus Is Risen!

Note for the Catechist

With this prayer service celebrate with your children the marvelous miracle of Jesus' resurrection. Prepare ahead of time some small cards (one for each child) cut in the profile of the risen Jesus with the words "Jesus is risen! Alleluia!" typed or printed on them. On your prayer table place a Bible (open to Jn 21), a candle, and the cards. (Optional: felt board with figures of Jesus, apostles, boat, and net against a background of blue sky and water and white sand.)

Opening Prayer

Catechist	Loving God, we rejoice because your Son Jesus is risen from the dead. His life brings us new life. Help us follow in Jesus' footsteps so we can one day join him in heaven. We ask this in Jesus' name.
All	Amen.

Scripture Reading

Catechist	As we read this gospel story, let's try to picture it. (Optional: move the felt figures to depict the story.)
Reader One	Just after daybreak Jesus stood on the beach. But the disciples didn't know it was Jesus. They had spent all night fishing and hadn't caught anything.
All	Jesus is risen. Alleluia!
Reader Two	Jesus said to them, "Have you caught any fish?" The disciples answered, "No." He told them, "Lower your net to the right side of the boat and you will find some." So they lowered the net. Now they could not lift it because there were so many fish.
All	Jesus is risen. Alleluia!
Reader Three	The disciple whom Jesus loved said to Peter, "It is the Lord!" When they had gone ashore, they saw a charcoal fire there with fish on it, and some bread.

Jesus said, "Bring some of the fish you have just caught." None of the disciples dared ask him, "Who are you?" They knew it was the Lord. Jesus took the bread and the fish and gave it to them. (Jn 21:4–14)

All   Jesus is risen. Alleluia!

Profession of Faith

Catechist   Let us proclaim our faith in Jesus. Do you believe in Jesus Christ who has redeemed us and is risen from the dead?

All   I do.

Catechist   Do you believe that through baptism Jesus has called us to be his disciples and to follow in his footsteps?

All   I do.

Catechist   Do you believe Jesus sent his Holy Spirit to help us grow in faith and love?

All   I do.

Catechist   Do you believe in the Catholic Church who teaches us in Jesus' name?

All   I do.

Catechist   May God bless us in the name of the Father and of the Son and of the Holy Spirit.

All   Amen.

Closing Prayer

Catechist   Loving God, you raised your Son Jesus, our Teacher and Savior, to be our salvation and our hope. Increase our faith in your love and help us follow Jesus each day of our lives. We ask this in Jesus' name.

All   Amen.

Closing Song
Jesus Christ Is Risen Today

Response
Hand out one of the "Jesus is risen" cards to each child as a reminder to think of Jesus during the Easter season.

Easter Egg Hunt
Have an Easter egg hunt. Use plastic eggs, and in each one put a piece of candy plus a slip of paper with an appropriate Scripture quote.

Gifts of the Spirit

Note for the Catechist

In celebration of the great feast of Pentecost, or any time during the year, use this prayer service to focus on the gifts of the Spirit. Prepare your prayer table with a Bible (open to Jn 15), a red candle, and a collage of pictures showing the gifts of the Spirit in action (persons studying, praying, helping one another, and so on). Point out the collage to the children before you begin the prayer service. Prepare red paper flames, one for each child, and write a gift of the Spirit on each.

Opening Prayer

Catechist   Holy Spirit, come into our hearts. Fill us with your gifts, and help us put them into practice.

All   Amen.

Scripture Reading

Reader One   Jesus said, "I have said all these things to you while I am with you. But the Advocate, the Holy Spirit, whom the Father will send in my name, will teach you everything. He will remind you of all that I have said to you. When the Spirit of truth comes, he will guide you in the truth. He will not speak on his own but will speak whatever he hears. He will glorify me, because he will take what is mine and declare it to you." (Jn 15:25–26; 16:13–14)

Responsorial Psalm

Invite the children to imitate the gestures.

Reader Two	The spirit of the Lord is upon me *(cross hands over heart)*.
All	The spirit of the Lord is upon me *(cross hands over heart)*.
Reader Three	The spirit of wisdom and understanding *(raise arms upward)*.
All	The spirit of the Lord is upon me *(cross hands over heart)*.
Reader Four	The spirit of counsel and might *(puts hands to head as if thinking)*.
All	The spirit of the Lord is upon me *(cross hands over heart)*.
Reader Five	The spirit of knowledge and the fear of the Lord *(clasp hands in prayer)*.
All	The spirit of the Lord is upon me *(cross hands over heart)*.

Reflection

Catechist — Let's each think a moment about the gifts the Spirit has given us. *(Pause.)* Look again at the pictures on the prayer table. What are some of the ways that we can put the gifts of the Spirit into action in our lives? *(Pause. Then invite the children to share their ideas. Younger children might prefer to draw.)*

Closing Prayer

Catechist — Loving God, you sent the Holy Spirit upon the apostles as they were united in prayer with Mary the mother of Jesus. Through her prayers, may your Spirit fill all people with love for you. We ask this in Jesus' name.

All — Amen.

Closing Song

Send Us Your Spirit, David Haas (G.I.A. Publications)

Response

Say together the gifts of the Spirit: wisdom, understanding, knowledge, counsel, fortitude, piety, and fear of the Lord. (Your religion text may use different names; if so, use them.) Then give out the red flames. Invite each child to pray for the gift on his or her flame.

Family Service

Encourage the children to talk with their families about a service project they can do together.

Come, Holy Spirit!

Note for the Catechist

In this prayer service children pray that the Spirit come to "renew the earth," including our hearts. Prepare your prayer table with a Bible (open to Acts 2), a red candle, and symbols of the Spirit (red flames, a dove, the number seven for the seven gifts, and so on). Prepare cutouts of a dove, one for each child.

Opening Prayer

Catechist	Loving God, your Spirit brings life and renews the whole earth. Send your Spirit into our hearts to fill us with the gifts of wisdom, courage, and love.
All	Amen.

Scripture Reading

Reader One	When the day of Pentecost had come, they were all together in one place. Suddenly from heaven there came a sound like the rush of a violent wind. It filled the entire house where they were sitting. Divided tongues, as of fire, appeared among them, and a tongue rested on each of them. All of them were filled with the Holy Spirit. (Acts 2:1–4)

Responsorial Psalm

Invite the children to imitate the gestures.

Reader Two	Bless the Lord, O my soul (*cross hands over heart*); O, Lord my God, you are very great (*raise arms upward*).
All	Lord, send forth your Spirit, and renew the face of the earth (*raise arms to heaven*).

Reader Three	You set the earth on its foundations *(lower arms down and out)* so that it shall never be shaken *(arms at side)*.
All	Lord, send forth your Spirit, and renew the face of the earth *(raise arms to heaven)*.
Reader Four	You make springs gush forth in the valleys *(raise arms up and apart like a fountain)*; they flow between the hills *(make a "wave" in the air)*.
All	Lord, send forth your Spirit, and renew the face of the earth *(raise arms to heaven)*.
Reader Five	The earth is full of your creatures *(open arms wide)*. When you open your hand, they are filled with good things *(open hands as if giving gifts)*.
All	Lord, send forth your Spirit, and renew the face of the earth *(raise arms to heaven)*. Prayer based on Psalm 104.

Closing Prayer

Catechist	Holy Spirit, cleanse and renew our hearts with your presence. May we be aware of your work within and around us. May we always be grateful for your gifts.
All	Amen.

Closing Song

The Spirit Is A-Movin', Carey Landry (OCP Publications)

Response

Give each child one of the doves you cut out. Tell them the dove is a reminder to ask the Holy Spirit to help them grow more like Jesus.

Create a Concert

Use music to explore a theme such as mission. Provide some different hymn books and old missalettes. Invite the group to search through them for songs that relate to mission. Then have the children prepare a concert in which they sing these songs, focusing on the chosen theme. Highlight the good work of the missions. You might even take an offering for a specific mission or project in your parish, diocese, or another country.

MAY

A Crown of Love

Note for the Catechist

This prayer service involves the children in a different kind of May crowning. Ask each child to bring a flower (real or drawn). Prepare a vase with water and a large piece of heavy cardboard with thumbtacks. If possible, provide prayer cards with a picture of Mary holding Jesus. Gather around the prayer table, prepared beforehand with the Bible, an image of Mary, and the vase. Prop the cardboard in front of the table.

Opening Prayer

Catechist	During May we honor Mary, the mother of Jesus and our mother. Mary loved God and other people very much. Let's ask Mary to pray for us, that we may grow in love.
All	Amen.

Scripture Reading

Reader One	The angel said, "Mary, God's favored one, you will have a son, Jesus." And Mary said, "I will do what God wants."
All	Mary, our mother, help us love God more every day.
Reader Two	Mary left home and went to help her cousin Elizabeth. Elizabeth said, "Blessed are you among women, and blessed is the child you will give birth to."
All	Mary, our mother, help us love our neighbor more every day.
Reader Three	Mary said, "My soul glorifies the Lord. I rejoice in God my savior, for he has done great things. Holy is God's name."
All	Mary, our mother, help us love God and our neighbor more every day.

Catechist	You've each brought a flower. Let your flower be a sign of a promise to Jesus and Mary—your promise to do something kind for others this week. Think for a moment about what you can do. Talk to Jesus and Mary about it. *(Allow a minute of quiet time.)* Now come up one at a time to place your live flower in the vase or your drawing on the cardboard. *(Play or sing a Marian hymn as the children bring up their flowers.)*

Litany of the Blessed Virgin

Catechist	(Invite the children to join you in praying the litany.) Father, Son, and Holy Spirit
All	Have mercy on us and bless us.
Catechist	Holy Mary
All	Pray for us.
Catechist	Holy Mother of God
All	Pray for us.
Catechist	Mother of divine grace
All	Pray for us.
Catechist	Mother most kind
All	Pray for us.
Catechist	Queen of heaven
All	Pray for us.
Catechist	Queen of martyrs
All	Pray for us.
Catechist	Queen of all saints
All	Pray for us.

Closing Song

Sing of Mary, Roland Palmer

Response

Give each child an image of Mary.

End of Year Activity

Ask the children for ideas about ways they can practice their faith with families and friends during the summer. Make a list with all their ideas. Photocopy it so you can give one to each child. Tell them to put a check next to each activity each time they carry it out (for example, help someone, go to church, say their morning prayers, read a good book).

THE PROFESSION OF FAITH

I Believe in One God

Note for the Catechist

This prayer service focuses on our belief in the one God and on God's name. On your prayer table place a Bible, a candle, and cards with different names for God (e.g., Adonai, Lord, God, Truth, Love, Creator, Shepherd, and so on). Arrange the cards artistically around the table, perhaps as place cards. There should be enough cards to have one for each child. You can even use different languages, especially if your parish includes various ethnic groups: Dios (Spanish), Dio (Italian), Dieu (French). On the back or inside of the cards type or print a short prayer or psalm verse.

Opening Prayer

Catechist   Loving God, we believe in you, we adore you, we trust you, we love you. Through the Bible and our religion lessons, through other people like our parents, we come to know more about you. Help us always know you better, so we can love you more. We ask this in Jesus' name.

All   Amen.

Gospel Reading

Reader   The man who had been cured of blindness answered, "Here is an astonishing thing! You do not know where this man comes from, and yet he opened my eyes. If this man were not from God, he could do nothing." [The leaders] answered him, "You were born entirely in sins, and are you trying to teach us?" And they drove him out.

Jesus heard that they had driven him out. When Jesus found the man, he said, "Do you believe in the Son of Man?" The man answered, "And who is he, sir? Tell me, so that I may believe in him." Jesus said to him, "You have seen him, and the one speaking with you is he." The man said, "Lord, I believe." And he worshiped Jesus. (Jn 9:30–38)

Responsorial Prayer

Reader One	"Hear, O Israel, the Lord our God is one Lord. You shall love the Lord your God with all your heart, and with all your soul, and with all your might." (Dt 6:4–5)
All	The Lord our God is one Lord.
Reader Two	"I am the God of Abraham, the God of Isaac, and the God of Jacob." (Ex 3:6)
All	The Lord our God is one Lord.
Reader Three	God said to Moses, "I am who I am. Say this to the people of Israel: 'I Am has sent me to you.'" (Ex 3:13–15)
All	The Lord our God is one Lord.
Reader Four	God is love and those who abide in love abide in God. (1 Jn 4:8)
All	The Lord our God is one Lord.
Reader Five	The Lord is my Shepherd, I shall not want. (Ps 23:1)
All	The Lord our God is one Lord.
Reader Six	The Lord is my light and my salvation. Whom shall I fear? (Ps 27:1)
All	The Lord our God is one Lord.

Closing Prayer

Catechist	Loving God, we praise and bless your name. We thank you for your steadfast love. Teach us your law, so we may keep it with all our hearts. We ask this in the name of Jesus your Son.
All	Amen.

Closing Song

For You Are My God, John Foley, SJ (OCP Publications)

Response

Before the closing song, bless the cards. Afterward, have the children come up. Give a card to each one.

Make a Mural

Have the children make a mural or collage with drawings and/or magazine cutouts that reflect their images of God and how God is at work in their lives.

God Cares for Us All

Note for the Catechist

In this prayer service we focus on the fact that we are all children of God, and need to respect and care for one another as God does for us. On your prayer table place a Bible, votive candles, and index cards, one for each child.

Opening Song

Beatitude People, Carey Landry (A Wonderful Song of Joy, OCP Publications)

Opening Prayer

Catechist   God of all people, you have made each of us in your image. Help us see your face in every person we meet. We ask this in Jesus' name.

All   Amen.

Guided Meditation

Catechist   Close your eyes and breathe in and out slowly. *(Pause.)* Picture yourself back in the time of Jesus. You see a big crowd of people and you want to know what is happening. Suddenly you see Jesus. He is talking to the people. Jesus says, "Do not worry about your life, what you will eat or what you will drink. Don't worry about what you will wear. Isn't life worth more than food, and the body more than clothing? Look at the birds of the air. They do not sow or reap or gather food into barns. But your heavenly Father feeds them. Aren't you worth more than they are? Your heavenly Father knows what you need." (Mt 6:25–33) Think about what Jesus just said. God cares about each of us. If he cares for the little birds and the fish and the lambs, how much more will he take care of us? *(Pause for a few minutes of silence.)*

Now let's pray for all the children around the world.

Intercessions

Reader One	Jenny is blind. She likes to feel and try new things and listen to music. Let's pray for the Jennys of this world.
All	Lord, bless all our sisters and brothers, your children.
Reader Two	Gary is autistic. He doesn't talk, but he smiles when you do something kind. Let's pray for all the Garys of this world.
All	Lord, bless all our sisters and brothers, your children.
Reader Three	Marci is in a wheelchair. She likes school, playing board games, and watching soccer and basketball. Let's pray for all the Marcis in the world.
All	Lord, bless all our sisters and brothers, your children.
Reader Four	Carl's family lives in a trailer in a poor section of town. His clothes are pretty shabby, and he looks sad sometimes. But Carl's a good friend. Let's pray for all the Carls of this world.
All	Lord, bless all our sisters and brothers, your children.
Reader Five	Caterina and her family have just moved to a new town. They don't speak English very well. Caterina wants to make friends but is finding it hard. Let's pray for all the Caterinas in this world.
All	Lord, bless all our sisters and brothers, your children.
Catechist	We all have a difficulty to overcome in our lives, whether it's physical, emotional, or spiritual. Let's help one another as Jesus would. Think for a few moments about how you could help one person in our group, especially if you find it hard to approach or to get along with this person.

(Pause for a few moments of silence.)

Response

Catechist	*(Hand out the index cards)* Write down the name of the person you thought of and one positive thing you could do for that person.

Closing Song

Every Person Is a Gift of God, Carey Landry (Hi God 3, OCP Publications)

Thanksgiving Dinner Collection

Ask the children to bring in nonperishable food items, plus frozen turkeys if you have the facilities to store them, to provide Thanksgiving dinner for folks in a local food pantry.

I Believe in Jesus

Note for the Catechist

In this prayer service we celebrate our belief in Jesus Christ, true God and true man. Prepare your prayer table with a Bible (open to Luke 2), a picture of Jesus and Mary, and a candle. Darken the room. If you're not allowed to light candles, use a spotlight or flashlights to shine on the table. If possible, have prayer cards of Jesus, one for each child.

Opening Song

Sing an appropriate song.

Opening Prayer

Catechist   Loving God, we believe that Jesus is truly your Son and also the son of Mary—both God and man. Help us be more like Jesus every day. We ask this in Jesus' name.

All   Amen.

Scripture Reading

Reader One   Joseph also went from the town of Nazareth in Galilee to Judea, to the city of David called Bethlehem. He went to be registered with Mary, to whom he was engaged and who was expecting a child. She gave birth to her firstborn son and wrapped him in bands of cloth. She laid him in a manger, because there was no place for them in the inn.

In that region there were shepherds living in the fields, keeping watch over their flock by night. Then an angel of the Lord stood before them, and the glory of the Lord shone around them. The angel said to them, "Do not be afraid; to you is born this day in the city of David a Savior, who is the Messiah, the Lord." (Lk 2:4–12)

All	Praise to you, Lord Jesus Christ!
Catechist	If we look in Scripture and our own lives, we can find a lot of titles to describe Jesus (some of which he used for himself and which we find in the gospels).

Litany

Reader Two	Lord of light, who overcomes our darkness and blindness
All	Have mercy on us, Jesus.
Reader Three	Good Shepherd, who leads us to green pastures and the fresh waters of your grace
All	Have mercy on us, Jesus.
Reader Four	Emmanuel, God-is-with-us, the Son who has been sent to bring us life
All	Have mercy on us, Jesus.
Reader Five	Our life and resurrection, you conquer sin and death
All	Have mercy on us, Jesus.
Reader Six	Jesus, our Way who leads to the Father
All	Have mercy on us, Jesus.
Reader Seven	Jesus, wisdom from on high, who teaches us the path of knowledge
All	Have mercy on us, Jesus.
Catechist	Let's spend a few moments to think about the mystery of Jesus who was God and who became one of us out of love for us.

Closing Song

Christ Be Beside Me, James D. Quinn, translator (OCP Publications)

Response

Hand out the pictures. Invite the children to keep them as a reminder to spend the day with Jesus.

Giving Tree

If your parish doesn't already have one, encourage the idea of a "giving tree." Parishioners bring in new, wrapped gifts with notes giving information about the appropriate age, gender, and size (for clothing). Then place the gifts under the tree. The gifts can be given to a poor parish in a mission area, or to needy families in your parish or city.

Mary, Jesus' Mother

Note for the Catechist

In this prayer service we honor Mary, Mother of God, the one who has brought into the world the Prince of peace. Prepare a prayer table with a Bible (open to Lk 1:26), a small statue of Mary holding Jesus, and a candle or flowers. Buy or make some cards, one for each child, with the Hail Mary printed on them.

Opening Song

Gentle Woman, Carey Landry (OCP Publications)

Opening Prayer

Catechist	Loving God, through the angel you asked Mary to be the mother of your Son. May we honor her as the Mother of Jesus, our Redeemer and Prince of peace.
All	Amen.

Scripture Reading

Reader One	God sent the angel Gabriel to a young girl named Mary. The angel said to her, "Greetings, favored one! You are special in God's sight. The Lord is with you."
All (bowing)	Hail Mary, the Lord is with you!
Reader Two	Mary wondered what the angel meant. The angel said, "Do not be afraid, Mary. You have found favor with God. You will have a son and you will name him Jesus. He will be called the Son of the Most High."
All (bowing)	Hail Mary, the Lord is with you!
Reader Three	Mary said to the angel, "How can this be, since I am not married?" The angel said, "The Holy Spirit will come upon you and the power of God will overshadow you. Your child will be holy and will be called Son of God." Then Mary said, "Here I am, the servant of the Lord. Let it be as you say." (Lk 1:26–38)
All (bowing)	Hail Mary, the Lord is with you!

Reflection

Pause for a few moments of silence, then reflect together. Explain to younger children any difficult words or passages.

- The angel's message to Mary changed her life. How?
- Do you ever hear messages from God in your heart or through other people? How do they change your life?
- What lesson can we learn from Mary? (how to say yes to God's love)
- With younger children ask them to draw a picture of Mary and the angel. Or you can bring old religious calendars with pictures of Mary, and let the children choose a picture and talk or write about it.

Intercessory Prayer

Catechist	God our Father wants us all to honor and imitate Mary, the mother of his Son. Now let us pray:
All	Mary, pray for us.
Catechist	Lord God, you brought Mary body and soul into heaven to share in Jesus' glory.
All	May we, too, share in that glory.
Catechist	You chose Mary to be our Mother too.
All	Through her prayers bring peace, salvation, and love to everyone.
Catechist	Mary is the Mother of the Church.
All	Through her prayers help us all turn to Jesus in times of need.

Closing Song

Yes, Lord, Yes, Carey Landry (Hi God 2, OCP Publications)

Response

Invite the children to take the cards home, and to pray often to Mary.

Make a Gospel or Saint Diorama

Set a large cardboard carton on its side, so the bottom of the box becomes the back of the scene. Decorate the outside of the carton by covering it with paper; then use paint or markers to draw a design. You can make the background of the scene by cutting out, drawing, or painting the scenery: grass, sky, mountains, a village, etc. You can glue small plastic trees and flowers, a small mirror for a lake, plastic animals, and so on. For figures to tell the gospel or saint's stories you can make paper cutouts, stick puppets, figures made out of dough, beads, yarn, pipe cleaners, or clothespins.

The Kingdom of Heaven

Note for the Catechist

Jesus taught about the kingdom in a special way through the Beatitudes. Prepare your table with a candle, flowers, a cushion or stand for the Bible, and cards with the Beatitudes printed on them, one for each child.

Begin with a procession to honor the Bible. Choose four of the children; you will follow them, then one of the tallest children will follow you, holding the Bible raised up. Ask this child to put the Bible in place, then open it to Mt 5. During the procession sing one of the following songs.

Procession Song

May Your Word, Paul Inwood (Children at Heart, OCP Publications)
Speak to Me, O Lord, Carey Landry (Hi God 5, OCP Publications)

Opening Prayer

Catechist	Jesus, in the beatitudes you taught us the way of the kingdom. May we seek this kingdom like the treasure in the field or the one fine pearl. Bless us always, Jesus.
All	Amen.

The Beatitudes

Use the suggested gestures and ask the children to do them with you. Practice ahead of time. Then during the prayer service, say the beatitudes together.

Blessed are the poor in spirit *(cross hands over heart)*

The kingdom of heaven is theirs *(hands reaching up)*

Blessed are those who mourn *(rub or wipe eyes as though crying)*

For they shall be comforted *(put arms together and rock as though rocking a baby)*

Blessed are the meek *(bow head slightly)*

For they shall inherit the earth *(spread arms open with hands open)*

Blessed are those who seek the right *(put right hand over heart as in a pledge)*

For they will be satisfied *(nod, smiling)*

Blessed are the merciful *(extend right hand as though offering friendship)*

For they will receive mercy *(sweep both hands back and hold to heart)*

Blessed are the pure in heart *(fold hands as in prayer)*

For they will see God *(raise arms up)*

Blessed are the peacemakers *(place hand over heart then extend out)*

For they will be called children of God *(place both hands over heart)*

Blessed are those who are persecuted *(put hands in front of face)*

For theirs is the kingdom of heaven *(raise arms up)*

Closing Prayer

Catechist   Loving God, we rejoice because we are invited to belong to your kingdom. We pray that everyone may listen to and hear the words of Jesus: "Come to me, for I am the way, the truth, and the life."

All   Amen.

Closing Song

Blest Are They, David Haas (GIA Publications)

Response

Invite the children to take the Beatitudes cards home and to read them often.

The Hunger Site

Visit the Hunger Site: www.hungersite.com.

   Click on Teacher's Resources in the left column. You will find information and activities to help educate your children about poverty in other countries. You can also click on America's Second Harvest, which is an activity you can do to provide food for the needy of our country.

Jesus Is Our Savior

Note for the Catechist

We celebrate the salvation Jesus brings each of us every day. On your prayer table place a crucifix, a candle, and a Bible (open to Jn 19:25). Make a paper cross for each child with the words: Jesus loves us.

Opening Song

Jesus Has Given His Life for Us, Carey Landry (Hi God 5, OCP Publications)

Opening Prayer

Catechist   God of love, you sent your Son Jesus to save us from sin and death. May we show our love as he did, by caring for our sisters and brothers. We ask this in Jesus' name.

All   Amen.

Scripture Reading

Reader One   Meanwhile, standing near the cross of Jesus were his mother, and his mother's sister, Mary the wife of Clopas, and Mary Magdalene. Jesus saw his mother and the disciple whom he loved standing beside her. He said to his mother, "Woman, here is your son." Then he said to the disciple, "Here is your mother." From that hour the disciple took her into his own home.

Reader Two   After this, when Jesus knew that all was now finished, he said, "I am thirsty." A jar full of sour wine was standing there. So they put a sponge full of the wine on a branch of hyssop. They held it to his mouth. When Jesus had received the wine, he said, "It is finished." Then he bowed his head and gave up his spirit. (Jn 19:25–30)

Guided Meditation

Catechist   Imagine that you are standing at the cross with Mary, Jesus' mother, with St. John, and with the other women. You are sad to see Jesus suffering. But you know that he promised he would rise again. Look at Jesus and make an act of faith and love. Promise you will try your best not to do anything that will make him and others suffer.

Intercessory Prayer

Catechist   God our Creator, hear the petitions we offer in the name of Jesus your Son. The response is "We pray to the Lord".

Reader Three   For the Church, the body of Christ: may she spread the good news of salvation throughout the world,

All   We pray to the Lord.

Reader Four   For families, may they find hope and love in the example of Jesus' sacrifice,

All   We pray to the Lord.

Reader Five   For all the sick, may they find strength and consolation in the cross of Jesus,

All   We pray to the Lord.

Reader One   For all of us here, may we trust in Jesus' love for us,

All   We pray to the Lord.

Closing Prayer

Catechist   God our Father, help us always remember your love for us. Forgive us for the times when we have turned away from your love. We ask this through Jesus your Son and our Savior.

All   Amen.

Closing Song

You Give Us Life, Christopher Walker (More Stories and Songs of Jesus, OCP Publications)

Response

Hand out the paper crosses, telling the children they are meant as reminders of Jesus' love for us. Suggest they carry the crosses with them.

Praying the Stations

At least once or twice during Lent, or even at other times of year, take the children to the parish church to pray the Stations of the Cross. (You may need the parents' permission if going to the church entails leaving the building and crossing the street.) Or pray the stations in your meeting space. You can announce each station, pause for silent prayer, then pray, "Jesus, through your cross and resurrection," while the children respond, "you have saved the world."

Stay with Us, Lord

Note for the Catechist

This prayer service celebrates Jesus' resurrection by telling the story of his appearance to the disciples traveling to Emmaus. On your prayer table place a Bible (open to Lk 24), a candle, flowers, and a loaf of bread (unsliced). Prepare cards in the shape of a loaf, with the words "Christ is risen!"

Opening Song

Christ the Lord Is Risen Today

Opening Prayer

Catechist	Jesus, you met the disciples on the road to Emmaus and broke bread with them. Be with us now as we pray together in your name.
All	Amen. Alleluia!

Scripture Reading

Catechist	As we read this gospel story, let's try to picture it.
Reader One	Now on that same day two of them were going to a village called Emmaus, about seven miles from Jerusalem. They were talking with each other about all these things that had happened. While they were talking and discussing, Jesus himself came near and went with them. But their eyes were kept from recognizing him. He said to them, "What are you discussing with each other while you walk along?"
All	Stay with us, Lord. Alleluia!

Reader Two	Then Jesus said to them, "Was it not necessary that the Messiah should suffer these things and then enter into his glory?" Then beginning with Moses and all the prophets, he interpreted to them the things about himself in all the Scriptures.
All	Stay with us, Lord. Alleluia!
Reader Three	When Jesus was at the table with them, he took bread, blessed and broke it, and gave it to them. Then their eyes were opened, and they recognized him. Jesus vanished from their sight. They said to each other, "Were not our hearts burning within us while he was talking to us on the road, while he was opening the scriptures to us?" (Lk 24:13–32)
All	Stay with us, Lord. Alleluia!
Catechist	Lord, you are with us as we bless and break this bread in your name. *(Bless the bread and pass it around for each child to take a piece.)*

Closing Prayer

Catechist	Jesus, we rejoice with the disciples and with the whole Church: Alleluia! The Lord is risen!
All	Alleluia! The Lord is risen!
Catechist	Jesus, be with us always. Alleluia!
All	Alleluia!
Catechist	Jesus, lay your hands on the sick and needy, and bless them. Alleluia!
All	Alleluia!

Closing Song

Alleluia, Christ Is Risen!, Carey Landry (Hi God 5, OCP Publications)

Response

Hand out the cards. Invite the children to keep them as a reminder that Jesus is with them.

Make a Banner

Make a banner with a eucharistic theme, either for the parish church or for your meeting space. Press the fabric (a light, solid color works best). Measure the size; make sure to cut on the grain. If you want to use a rod, add four inches to the height of the fabric. Using stencils or designs penciled onto tissue paper, cut letters and shapes from various materials. Lay out the entire banner. Use straight pins to hold everything in place before sewing or using glue to attach them. Rearrange as needed and secure the pieces to the background.

I Believe in the Holy Spirit

Note for the Catechist

In this prayer service we pray that the Spirit of love may dwell in our hearts and enable us to bear the fruits of love. Prepare your prayer table with a Bible (open to Gal 5), a red candle, and red roses (the symbol of love), one for each child. On each rose write: The fruit of the Spirit is love.

Opening Song

The Spirit Is A-Movin', Carey Landry (Hi God! OCP Publications)

Opening Prayer

Catechist   Holy Spirit, come fill our hearts and minds with your love. Show us how to follow Jesus every day. Make us strong when we are faced with a choice between right and wrong.

All   Amen.

Guided Meditation

Catechist   Close your eyes and breathe slowly and gently. We are going to make a trip back in time to the day of Pentecost. Picture yourself with Mary and Jesus' disciples in the Upper Room. We're all gathered together, praying for the coming of the Holy Spirit, as Jesus asked us to pray. Suddenly there is a tremendous wind. It seems to fill the whole house. You feel it in your hair and across your face. It's a powerful feeling.

Then you see little flames in the shape of tongues. There is one of these flames over the head of each of the people there. What is happening? you wonder. The Holy Spirit whom Jesus promised to send to his disciples fills your heart with love and courage. Some of the disciples begin to speak in different languages. A crowd gathers outside, people from all the known world.

How do you feel about all this? Reflect a moment, then draw a picture, or write a poem or your own description of what has happened.

Responsorial Psalm

Reader One	The fruit of the Spirit is love, joy, peace, patience, kindness, generosity, faithfulness, gentleness, and self-control.
All	The fruit of the Spirit is love.
Reader Two	If we live by the Spirit, let us also be guided by the Spirit.
All	The fruit of the Spirit is love.
Reader Three	Bear one another's burdens, and in this way you will fulfill the law of Christ.
All	The fruit of the Spirit is love.
Reader Four	If you sow to the Spirit, you will reap eternal life from the Spirit. So let us not grow weary in doing what is right, for we will reap at harvest time.
All	The fruit of the Spirit is love. (Gal 5)

Closing Prayer

Catechist	Come, Holy Spirit, with your gifts and the fruits of your love. May we put these fruits into practice each day of our lives.
All	Amen.

Closing Song

God Make My Life a Little Light, Jack Miffleton (God Be in My Heart)

Response

Give the children each a rose as a reminder that they are temples of the Spirit.

Let a Little Love Shine

Suggest to the children that they think of ways they can spread the Spirit's gift of love. You might want to give them a list of books they can read; for example, a book on the saints, books on caring for others, and so on.